Sand Tiger Sharks

by Grace Hansen

Abdo
SHARKS
Kids

abdopublishing.com

Published by Abdo Kids, a division of ABDO, PO Box 398166, Minneapolis, Minnesota 55439.

Copyright © 2016 by Abdo Consulting Group, Inc. International copyrights reserved in all countries. No part of this book may be reproduced in any form without written permission from the publisher.

Printed in the United States of America, North Mankato, Minnesota.

102015

012016

Photo Credits: Alamy, iStock, Seapics.com, Shutterstock, Thinkstock, ©User:timsacton / CC-SA-2.0 p.15

Production Contributors: Teddy Borth, Jennie Forsberg, Grace Hansen

Design Contributors: Laura Mitchell, Dorothy Toth

Library of Congress Control Number: 2015941984

Cataloging-in-Publication Data

Hansen, Grace.

 Sand tiger sharks / Grace Hansen.

   p. cm. -- (Sharks)

ISBN 978-1-68080-154-5 (lib. bdg.)

Includes index.

1. Sand tiger shark--Juvenile literature.   I. Title.

597.3/3--dc23

                    2015941984

Table of Contents

Sand Tiger Sharks 4

Food & Hunting 16

Baby Sand Tiger Sharks 18

More Facts 22

Glossary 23

Index 24

Abdo Kids Code. 24

Sand Tiger Sharks

Sand tiger sharks live in many oceans. They are found almost everywhere. They do not live in the eastern Pacific Ocean.

Sand tigers prefer warm waters. They spend most of their time near shore.

Sand tigers are mostly brownish-gray. Their bellies are white. They have spots on their backs.

9

Sand tigers look different from other sharks. Their noses are cone-shaped. Their teeth poke out of their mouths.

Sand tigers look very scary. But they are not known to be **aggressive**.

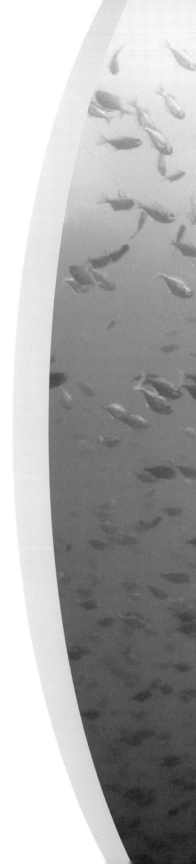

Sand tigers have two big dorsal fins. Their caudal fins are also large.

dorsal fins

caudal fin

15

Food & Hunting

Sand tigers sometimes hunt in groups. They mostly eat small fish. They also eat crabs and squid.

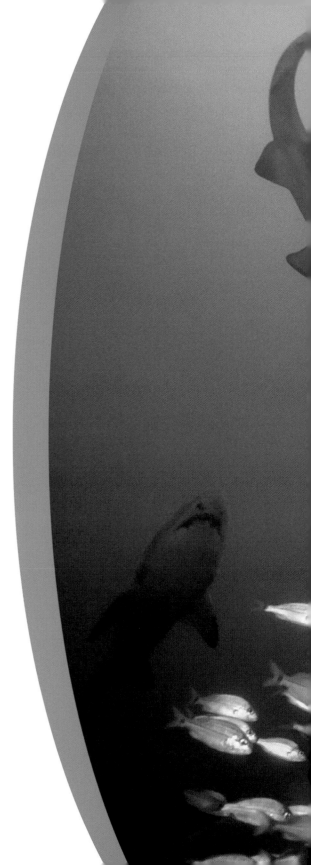

Baby Sand Tiger Sharks

Sand tigers give birth to live young called pups. Pups begin as eggs inside of the mother. Some grow faster than others.

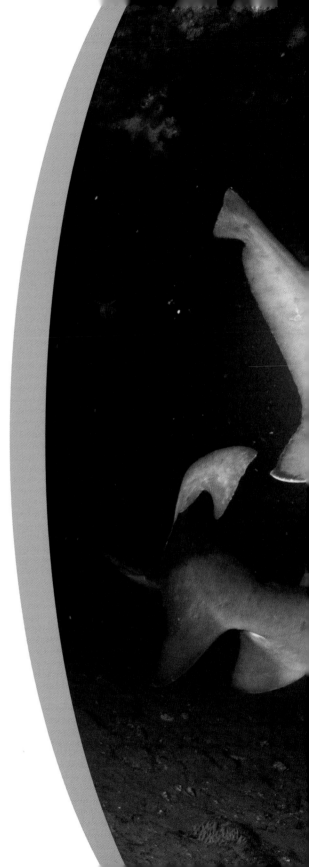

19

Two pups hatch before the rest.
They eat the other eggs before
they are born. The two pups
are on their own after birth.

21

More Facts

- Sand tiger sharks swallow air. They hold the air in their stomachs. This is so they can float motionless in the water.

- "Sand" is in their name because they like to be in shallow water near shore. "Tiger" is in their name because they really like to eat!

- Because only two pups survive to birth, sand tiger sharks have the lowest birth numbers of any shark.

Glossary

aggressive – ready or likely to attack.

caudal fin – the tail fin of a shark.

dorsal fin – the triangular fin on the back of a shark.

Index

color 8

eggs 18, 20

fins 14

food 16, 20

habitat 4, 6

hunting 16

mouth 10

nose 10

Pacific Ocean 4

pups 18, 20

teeth 10

abdokids.com

Use this code to log on to abdokids.com and access crafts, games, videos, and more!

Abdo Kids Code:
SSK1545